BOOK OF POETRY

First Published in the United Kingdom April 2016

1st Edition

Published by Stamford Independent Publishing

Printed by BJ's Print & Design, Unit 5, Gwash Way Ind Est, Ryhall Rd, Stamford, PE9 1XP

ISBN: 978-0-9935994-0-8

Thanks to all who have contributed poems and helped make this book possible. To Karen Burrows and Bill Taylor for whipping all the poets into shape, to Ricky Duff and Andy Croft for help editing and to James Baguley for putting the book together in his spare time.

Special thanks to Stamford Arts Centre and South Kesteven District Council for coughing up the money for printing this book, hopefully we will sell enough copies to pay you back.

INTRODUCTION

In April 2012, the Arts Centre programmed the first Verse Festival, a small scale poetry festival for the town. It was a tentative start, but an artistic sucess. Nevertheless, out of small seeds grew great things.

It was decided that it was about time that Stamford had its very own Poet Laureate. This has been a role that has continued to evolve over the years and we have been so lucky in having had some wonderful poets take up the mantle and work hard at raising the profile of poetry in town. Next to follow was the start of our monthly Cellar Bar gathering of local poets called, not very originally, Pint of Poetry. In the early days, often only one or two poets would turn up to read but in time and through word of mouth, the popularity of this event has grown and grown. We have a loyal and very talented group of poets who brave all weathers to meet up and share their love of the written word over pint or two.

I am immensely proud of the thriving poetry scene that we now have in Stamford and the fact that we are now, in 2016, holding our 3rd Verse Festival, which continues to grow in strength and range. The quality of the work we listen to at Pint of Poetry month by month certainly deserves to be enjoyed by a wider audience and it was because of this that the idea of The Stamford Book of Poetry was born. Included in the book are poems by most of our regulars, all local to Stamford. I hope you will enjoy reading them as much as I have enjoyed listening to them.

Karen Burrows
Arts Centre Administrator and Frustrated Poet

* * * * * * * *

Back in 2012 there was a poetry competition prepared and run by Stamford Arts Centre, in order to find a Poet Laureate for Stamford, who was expected to work for one year alongside the Mayor. This had never been done before and it was not known what the outcome would be.

It was at this time with two weeks to go until the deadline, that a friend of mine said I should enter the competition. Having never recited my poetry before I was very nervous and wondered why anyone would actually want to listen. However, the theme was 'Dreams' and I had nothing to lose. The competition went ahead and I was lucky enough to become the first Stamford Poet Laureate, a position that should not be taken lightly.

The year of 2012 was a particularly busy year for the whole of the UK, due to the Olympics and the

Diamond Jubilee of Queen Elizabeth II. The Mayor's diary was full of events which in turn gave the Poet Laureate a responsibility to write poetry. It was an exciting time for all poets in and around Stamford. We were going to try and engage others in poetry and encourage the 'bedroom poets' into the lime light.

Burghley House held its first screening of the Olympics and the Olympic Torch sped it's way through our streets, which gave way for another chance to express views through the medium of poetry. The Cellar Bar opened its doors allowing poets to demonstrate their skill at 'Pint of Poetry' nights and the Stamford Arts Centre allowed poets to hold a monthly forum. The seeds had been sown, and poetry in Stamford was on the map.

Becoming the first Poet Laureate of Stamford opened many doors. It was a fantastic year in which I made new friends, learned a lot about myself, gained confidence in my writing, presentation, performance and the chance to listen to other poets expressing their thoughts, ideas and critics through this medium. 'Ut diu ut permanere'

Darren Rawnsley
First Poet Laureate of Stamford

CONTENTS

INTRODUCTION 3

ABOUT THE POETS 9

DARREN RAWNSLEY

Down in the Cellar 16
The Runner 18
She Waited 20
A Flash in the Pan - Scarborough 21

TERESA McLEAN

Red Kite 23
Stamford 25

BILL TAYLOR

First World War Love Story 27
In Rememberance of an Eight Year Old Hero 29
Seasons in Stamford 31
Inspiration 34

REBECCA WESTWOOD

I Wasn't There 35
A Life in my Stamford Town 38
Differences 41
The Spanish Steps 44

CARDINAL COX

Stamford Stones 46
Sir Robert's Tomb, St. Mary's Stamford 47

CONTENTS

William Stukeley 48
Robert Owen 49

JOHN LEAROYD

When Time Runs Out (the Realisation) 50
The Stander 52
Not Every Soldier (the Reality) 54

PHIL DUNKERLEY

Amoral Story 56
The Man of Trust 57
Name and Number 58
Lichens 59

CAMILLA McLEAN

They All go to M & S 60
The San Antonio Sonnet 61
XYZ 62
Musings on Wee 64

RICHARD BARTER

Stagefright 65
Threading the Needle 67
Mating Game 69
Penelope 71

JOE HOTEN

Fair Enough 73
Least Fun on the hill 76

CONTENTS

WENDY McLEAN

Ode to Amethyst 79
I Know About You 80
Liberty, Equality, Fraternity 83

CHIN TAN

Credo (or Stupidity) 86
La Vieille Dame sans Cerveau 87
Liberty 90
Grammar 92

MIKE ALDERSON

Patron 93
Walking Backwards 94
Stanley 95
Reading Time 96

JIMMY PEA

The Death of Daniel Lambert aged 39 97
Curiosity Killed the Cat 100
Owl-me 102
Curb Scrawlin' 105

ANDREW CROFT

What is the Point in a Wasp? 106
Man Flu 107
White Van Driver 109
Myths & Legends of Stamford Town 110

ABOUT THE POETS

DARREN RAWNSLEY

When Darren rode out of Yorkshire, hung up his flat cap, gave the Whippet to a good home and turned on the heating instead of putting another piece of coal on the fire, there was nothing left but to write poetry. As the first Stamford Poet Laureate he began to put pen to paper and 'ee-bah gum' has kept going.

TERESA McLEAN

Teresa is mum to three and has grandchildren and one great grandson. She was Stamford's second poet laureate and still helps promote poetry locally. She is also a singer/songwriter, enjoys creative sewing, gardening and helping out at a local charity shop.

BILL TAYLOR

Bill has been writing poetry for many years and was Stamford Poet Laureate from 2014 to 2015. He likes to write "of the moment" poetry about current affairs and issues, especially if they involve ranting or ridiculing politicians and journalists. He currently performs somewhere around the area every week and organises evenings of live music and spoken word entertainment in local pubs.

ABOUT THE POETS

REBECCA WESTWOOD

Rebecca was the fourth Stamford Poet Laureate from 2015 to 2016. She has been writing poetry since school, throughout university and into adulthood. Poems such as 'Differences' come from losing her dad to Motor Neurone Disease and the heartache involved. Poetry for her is a friend, a medium, a passion and a tool for reflection on life.

PETE 'CARDINAL' COX

Cardinal Cox's work has been published in the small-press for around thirty years. He is currently poet-in-residence for The Dracula Society, and developing a "spooken" word show, 'High Stakes'.

JOHN LEAROYD

An ex-soldier and former residential social worker who specialises in writing poetry and prose concerning conflicts since WW1, John's writing is powerfully realistic and pulls no punches. He has performed across the east Midlands and covers the current situations in Syria, Afghanistan and the refugee crises in his ongoing work.

ABOUT THE POETS

PHIL DUNKERLEY

Phil is an active member of poetry groups in south Lincolnshire, where he lives, and Cambridgeshire. His poems have appeared in anthologies, journals and magazines, and on websites, and he has also translated poems from Spanish into English.

CAMILLA McLEAN

Camilla, an advertising copywriter by trade, draws on popular culture and her poetry has been described as replete with acerbic observations and light but not slight. She loves to perform her own peculiar brand of poetry in pubs and on street corners, much to the bemusement of passers-by.

RICHARD BARTER

Richard started writing poetry only a year or so ago. He had time on his hands and nothing better to do, but then is there anything better to do?

JOE HOTEN

Joe is a twenty-something-year-old writer and musician from Stamford, actively involved in the respective local scenes. He sees himself as somewhere between a compassionate misanthrope and a cynical humanitarian.

WENDY McLEAN

Wendy has been writing poetry since the age of 10. She writes from personal experiences and reflects on things that strongly affect her thoughts at the time she writes.

CHIN TAN

Though he trained and worked as a structural engineer, has always been keen on music and poetry. He thinks a good poem should be melodious to the ear, and good music has to be poetic at heart.

MIKE ALDERSON

Mike was born in Tanzania, lived in Bexhill, Derby, Durham, Maidstone, Bristol and now in the Deepings. His pet rabbit died a few years ago and frogs have returned to his pond.

JAMES 'JIMMY PEA' PARKER

Jimmy was challenged to enter the first Stamford Poet Laureate competition just over 5 years ago. He hadn't written any poems up until that point, but he rose to the challenge and wrote his first poem. He didn't win, he probably came third, out of three, but it sparked something off and he ended up joining the Pint of Poetry every month and wrote three or four new poems for each session. He then went away and had two children and the poetry became as rare as a decent nights' sleep.

ANDREW CROFT

Andy bought his first guitar in his teens and started writing songs with humorous and strange subject matter. Eventually he moved on to writing songs whose lyrics stand alone as poems. Andy has run the Cellar Bar at the Arts Centre, where Stamford Pint of Poetry is held, for twenty years. He is a Chemist, a Musician, and recently a Town Councillor.

POEMS

DOWN IN THE CELLAR

Step in through the doorway, step down to the cellar
and converse with the patrons, these amiable fellows,
who talk about poetry, songs from the seventies
and how Posh would have won if it had gone over to
penalties.
A bar where the staff always give of their best
while the hard working person comes in for a rest
and a drink to unwind to think and to ponder,
perhaps even find an old friend from back yonder;
then sit, have a drink, could be soda and lime,
give a toast to the landlord on his fifth glass of wine,
as he collects his guitar and sings from the heart,
the Cellar Bar welcoming right from the start
of the evening to last orders, for all kinds of folk.
Far across borders of England they come,
to play on the fiddle or beat on the drum.
To read poetry and prose, or tell a tall tale,
to munch on pork scratching and drink down some ale,
be it Guinness or bitter, wine or champagne,
the cellar bar treats all its patrons the same,
with no airs or graces, a smile on all faces;
something you don't find in too many places.
The promise of festivals in the following year,
marquees and mics and all of the gear
needed to ensure the perfect of days,
while Andy's tenth bottle puts him into a haze.
He stands and is counted along with the greats,
running the bar, helps organise fetes,

with loads of support from the regular drinkers,
the poets, musicians, writers and thinkers.
So stay for a while and chat to a friend,
drink and be merry until in the end,
it is time to depart, the key locks the door,
and the night makes the Cellar Bar silent once more.

Darren Rawnsley
Stamford Poet Laureate 2012 - 13

THE RUNNER

The darkness is gone, now the sun burns my eyes
As I trudge through the desert with another disguise,
I hear him behind me on a steed of light grey
whose muscles compound whilst heading my way.

Faster and faster my blood flies around
through the open blue rivers down chambers
that sound, like double bass drums pounding my ears,
Glimpses of sweat washed over with tears.

I rip up my body for freedom and speed
his hooves and his rider, those arrogant thieves
who steal my possessions, my will and my life,
They give me back nothing but sharpen the knife.

Now I am naked way over the dune
the walls are enclosing, there isn't much room
to manoeuvre and run, I just slip in the mud
the walls of my trench collapse as they should
while the torrent descends making heavy my steps,
He is standing beside me, above me behind me
I am not quite lost yet

The river runs slower his hold is unkind
But there lies a softness somewhere deep behind
his rusty old armour his nicotine scent,
I turn and squeeze through a narrow dark vent,

No light at the end, no help to be seen
I fall off the curb and awake from the dream,
once again it is real, a punch then the scream!

Darren Rawnsley
Stamford Poet Laureate 2012 - 13

SHE WAITED

She waited for a message from a loved one who had gone so long ago, but not forgotten. Stuck in memory, locked away with thoughts of thank you, and the gladness that was poured upon her family.

She waited for a message, but the medium was not looking, gave no clue of what was happening, who was coming, who was going? No way of knowing.

She waited for a message as the clock ticked by the minutes "I have lady", said the medium, "her name is sort of cloudy, but I think it could be Mabel, she has passed away quite recent".

She waited for a message as the clairvoyance was ending and again the disappointment, showed the Spirit Guides ascending onto other people waiting, her turn had not been taken.

She waited for a message on the walk across the meadows to her own front door in shadows and a heated cup of coffee, when she heard a quiet whisper, whilst she sat upon the sofa, " I am here and I am happy"!

Darren Rawnsley
Stamford Poet Laureate 2012 - 13

A FLASH IN THE PAN - SCARBOROUGH

The fingers of the sea reach out and stretch their palms upon the rocks where seagulls hang around like teenagers near the corner shop, who chat and grab a bite to eat of crab or mussel, then shout hello, the annoying cry, and greet you on Scarborough's vast and twisting cliff where Victorians used to live and walk on sunny days. Perambulators moving slowly, long skirts and hats and stripy swimsuits, boldly walking into waters deep.

Children's voices echoing the days gone by with spades and buckets swinging, sounds of one Direction singing through earphones loud enough to damage tiny drums and heard by relaxers in the sun who beg for peace and wish the breeze would just die down a little more, so that sand would stay upon the floor and not get into egg and mayonnaise or up your nose and any other place the sand explores.

The smell of fish and chips encourages the visitors to sit with tray in hand as tomato sauce drips onto dust and dirty sand while the boats and yachts set sail to skirt the coast and share with those who want to try a different lifestyle, most of all give way to dreams.

Homes and houses where a guest can stay, coloured walls that pave the way high upon the Scarborough shore, blue, and yellow, pink and more beg the visitor to come through the open door and share a

breakfast fit for kings, a hearty way to start a new
exciting day that brings out laughter on the ghost
train ride, or riding on the wheel, no way to hide
your fear of heights. All money spent on two pence
slots where more and more toys will block the way
for kids to get a drop of coin to help them carry
on and run from one machine to try their luck on
horse racing or hook the duck, the sound of bingo
calling two fat ladies, win a prize, cockles, mussels,
no surprise to watch the passers by stuff their faces,
again the sand gets into places it should never reach
and you're not even sat upon the golden sandy
beach.
But look across from South to North and witness
sights you would've never thought existed, where
twisting coast leads your eyes to Scarborough
Castle, proud and buildings listed to preserve their
ancient historic beauty. I encourage you to visit and
sit a while, take in the views and see how locals share
a smile and seagulls shout a welcome call then go
and fill your bag with rock and all that Scarborough
has to offer and enjoy the fayre.

Darren Rawnsley
Stamford Poet Laureate 2012 - 13

RED KITE

It was the colour that caught my eye,
a blip of scarlet against the blue.
The kite hung there like a child's drawing,
perfect, right down to the multicoloured
bows weighting the tail.
Of it's earthbound flyer there was no sign,
the string too fine to see, to follow by eye,
to lead me to the person whose pull
kept it floating.
The field below was empty.
Someone with local knowledge
must have tied it down,
to tug against a thermal,
to fly as if by magic.

Further across the sky
two black silhouettes, menacing,
like a child's drawing of a nightmare.
Closer they flew and closer,
until, caught in the sunlight,
their plumage shone russet red.
Riding the warm air they circled,
 inspecting their namesake,
up and up, undersides of wings
as white as angels.
Closer they flew and closer,
until a wing brushed the unseen string.

The toy jinked and bobbed.
Leisurely they flew away,
Owning the air.

Teresa McLean
Stamford Poet Laureate 2013 - 14

STAMFORD

This is the place to the west of the fen
Where the stolid women and quiet men
Farm and hunt that they might eat
As the Romans march up Ermine Street.

This is the place at the waters edge,
The last place to cross before the sedge,
Where they kept the skill of the potter's wheel,
Learned to trade, learned to deal.

This is the place where a town has grown,
A town decreed from king Edgar's throne
To be a Borough, and with four more
Make a network, serve the Danelaw.

This is the town grown bigger yet
On spinning and weaving the haberget
With pack train and wagon to carry the load
And a castle built for the Great North Road.

This is the town of the mid-lent fair
When crusaders swooped on the traders there
The blood of the Jews ran onto the street
As they died where they fell at the soldiers feet.

This is the town grown rich on wool,
Where there is time to sport at running the bull,
With fourteen churches to praise the Lord
For the wealth of the town built at the stone ford.

This is the town where Henry the Eighth
Sent Dr. London's men to the friars gates,

Black, Grey, White and Austin friar
All turned from their land at the king's desire.

This is where Cecil, Secretary of State,
Acquired land for a large estate,
Made his plans and had them fulfilled,
A great house that took thirty-three years to build.

This is where Cromwell's troops rode down
Besieging Burghley and searching the town
For the fugitive king, they searched in vain,
Soon his son was restored to reign.

This is the town the Georgians made
With an assembly room where the wealthy played.
With no industry on which to rely
and the north/south train line passed it by.

This is the town where the flying corps
Learned their skills and went to war.
And from here the RAF "Brylcreem Boys"
One hundred and fifty one planes destroyed.

This is the town that is the best
Or so we are told by the Sunday press.
All those histories come and gone
Still the golden stones go dreaming on.

Teresa McLean
Stamford Poet Laureate 2013 - 14

FIRST WORLD WAR LOVE STORY

He sits surrounded -

Mud, blood, persistent thud
Of mortars blasting his trench.
Tearless tommies huddle in dogholes
Scribbling letters amongst the stench,
To girls who sit at home, lost, lonely souls.
Mustard gas creeps silent, death
For those slow to fit their masks;
Coughing out their final breath
As Kitchener back in Blighty asks
For more young men to go to France.
Six weeks of living in dire conditions
Before they're killed or maimed.
This is their version of perdition.
Every night's the same game,
Lure the sniper, duck the shells,
Surely this is worse than Hell.

She sits alone -

Hollow eyes and tear stained cheeks;
He's been away for several weeks.
He said he'd write to her each day
But not a word since he went away.
That day in March they kissed farewell,
He said "Don't fret dear, all will be well,

Before you know it I'll be back,
This war won't last and that's a fact"
But in her heart of hearts she knew
That those who'll return unscathed are few.
Her silent prayers that he stay safe and sound
Are all in vain; as six days in he climbed a mound;
The German bullet found its mark,
His broken body rots in the dark.
She'll never see him home again,
She'll never feel a love the same.
She sits alone and wonders why
Her man, and millions more must die.

Bill Taylor
Stamford Poet Laureate 2014 - 15

IN REMEMBRANCE OF AN EIGHT YEAR OLD HERO

Gripping the handlebars between my father's hard hands;
Perched precariously on the tiny crossbar seat,
Wind whipping my ears, eyes watering, I loved the thrill
Of those rickety rides and couldn't wait,
Desperately couldn't wait to ride on my own,
Ride my own bike, be a big boy;
Career, careless, legs pumping metal pedals
Until my thighs hurt; skidding on the dirt tracks
Round the edge of the Park, screaming in the dark
To scare the girls as we fly by, smug with power.
A bike, garishly painted, seven and sixpence
From the cattle market, second hand,
But did I dare complain? Did I care?
Independent at last, I was off, storming the streets,
Bursting up bridges to fly, free-wheeling on the downward slope.
No hills in Peterborough
But we made do with gentle slopes and
Risky rampages along the river bank for our thrills.
To Orton Staunch, to cross to the South side,
The dangerous unknown of Stanground and Fletton,
Where strange accents shouted cheerily across the roads,
Or out on the tracks through the farm fields
That now are known as Netherton and Bretton.

My bike opened up a new wide world
Along whose paths and lanes I hurled headlong
In search of adventure, Dan Dare on a bike,
Tarzan the Bikeman, Davy Crockett on his trusty steed.
Now I had my own bike, I could be a hero,
An eight year old hero, but a hero indeed.

Bill Taylor
Stamford Poet Laureate 2014 - 15

SEASONS IN STAMFORD

Cobbles shine slippery wet as Winter storms lash down;
Shoppers scurry for cover through the dripping town.
Small boys splash in puddles before their lift from school
Water spattered windows sparkle like bright jewels.

The river rises rapidly across the flood plain;
Trees bend to the wind and drip with heavy rain.
Wool sodden sheep shuffle under hedgerows
Cats trip through sodden gardens on their tippy toes.

Rain turns to snow in the icy cold gales,
White Collyweston roofs look more like sails
on stone ships. Postmen plough up paths with mail,
Footprints in the snow create a crazy trail.

* * * * * * * *

Snowdrops proudly poke petals through thawed earth;
Birdsong brightens mornings, as Spring sun creates
rebirth.
Greening trees and church spires spike the April skies,
Mowers motors start up now the grass has dried.

White clouds scud through skies bright blue,
Friday markets sell garments of every style and hue,
Sun glints gold on the church clock of St Mary's;
Pigeons pout and strut, while smaller birds look wary.

Stamford Spring sees daffodils dot the river brink,
St George's churchyard may trees brightly blossom pink,
Short sleeved shirts replace jackets and scarves
As Stamford shows it does nothing by halves.

* * * * * * * *

Honey-coloured stone shimmers in the Summer sun.
Mayflies meander on the river margins, sweating mums
Push baby buggies up sloping passageways,
As light fades, following yet another fruitful day.

Young lovers stroll leisurely along,
Sparrows break into their evening song,
Drinkers clink glasses outside The Jolly Brewer;
Sunset over the Meadows, beauty true and pure.

The river ripples gently in the evening breeze
Cows are grazing, donkeys dozing all along the leas.
Anglers crouch contentedly, casting envious glances
At kingfishers spearing the surface, beaks like lances.

* * * * * * * *

Burghley boughs burn brown and Autumn gold;
Starlings gather ready to escape the cold.

Hanging basket flowers fade, look so tired;
Logs are sawn before wood burners fired.

Evenings shorten and bonfires burn
Ladies in the Cosy Club before their return
From early Christmas shopping in Sheepmarket
Would have come in the car but couldn't park it.

Stamford wraps up, preparing for winter cold
Wellies and winter coats are now starting to be sold.
No matter what the season, Stamford is the place to live.
What other town in England has quite so much to
give?

Bill Taylor
Stamford Poet Laureate 2014 - 15

INSPIRATION

Three quick small steps to his one steady pace,
I wanted to stay by his side, look up and see his face,
Not trail behind, dogged follower, in his wake;

My father was not a big man, not a strong man,
But he was the man to inspire me, fire my imagination
With his words, his tales, his love of Shakespearean
quotation.
The power and resonance of his voice could hold an
audience in thrall,
All spellbound by his presence, his deep brown
baritone,
And I was not alone. Many a young mind would find
Itself determined to succeed, achieve, believe his creed
That you must set yourself the highest goals, aim for
the stars,
The whole world is yours; see how far you can go,
Show others what you can do, through determination
and hard graft.
I laugh with him now, pretending everything is fine,
knowing the truth;
Three quick small gasps to my one steady breath,
I want to stay by his side, look down and see his face,
So frail and fragile now, as he approaches death.

Bill Taylor
Stamford Poet Laureate 2014 - 15

I WASN'T THERE

Written for Remembrance Sunday 2015

I wasn't there,
don't remember the smell of mud
caked under my fingernails

listening to my heart
wrench itself under my ribs,
so loud
I could almost taste
the blood pumping
with my
in
and
out
breathe

I didn't feel gunshots
resonant
under my skin.

I didn't float above and below masses of water
listening out for an unseen menace

or stretch my eyes across the horizon waiting
for them to come.

I didn't watch
aeroplanes litter the sky
on missions of destruction.

I didn't feel the weight of the animal's eye fall upon
me as I asked
much of its loyalty as it stepped out into the
unknown beside me.

I wasn't there,

didn't sacrifice
my brethren,
strangers,
comrades
alone but bound together
by the common goal.

I didn't watch some take their last
shaken,
scared
breathe.

Die.

I didn't feel the pride of uniform,
fear of death,
of defeat.
I am here,

hearing the stories,
listening intently to the memories.

I am left instead with history,
dates,
encouraged to remember the facts,
the sentiments

so we can remember them,

so we do not repeat this tar on ours
and everybody else's history.

I wasn't there

but I promise I
and my children
will remember them.

Rebecca Westwood
Stamford Poet Laureate 2015 -16

A LIFE IN MY STAMFORD TOWN

A cacophony of geriatric buildings,
present modern angles, words
etching themselves across the horizon,
tingling my eyelids.

Like a painter I see these colours, these edges,
its beauty is absorbed into my heart
as I incline upon the Great North Road.

The finest view twixt Edinburgh and London
awaited me
with a knowing of the history of its secrets.

I rest, momentarily,
under the wooden beams,
following in the steps of Royalty,
nobility,
the lawmen and the lawless,
all of us seeking the answer to the question
that never changes.

I taste the air
full of promise.

The river sweeping its way through the town
laden with sights long gone, its scars washed anew
like its people.

A peace of mind
passion in silence
of observation.

The presence is a gift.

The giggle of a child
echoes through the meadows like a charm.

The call of a lady to her dog
resonates like a spell of connection,

she doths her leather rimmed hat
at the lovers
preening on the picnic table,
pulling her tweed coat tightly against her skin
to keep out the cold.

The spaniel listens intently for a whistle,
a direction,
a call to return to the streets
where the revellers cover the pavement
with their colourful steps
hoping to be transported to a happier plain.

The presence is a gift.
I see it.

I feel it.

I sit by the fire
throwing its flickering dance over the stone walls
that try to enclose me,
smile,
I am no bird in a cage

I seek a life

troubled just the same as
every body
choosing whether to ignore
or ponder upon it.

I seek an answer to my own question
in my Stamford town.

Rebecca Westwood
Stamford Poet Laureate 2015 -16

DIFFERENCES

Words. Words. Words

You are a gold nugget, I am gold dust,
rich.
Both priceless, one produced by the other,
one bigger, bolder, stronger.
You were strong, lifting me onto your shoulders,
a little face at the zoo cooing at the wild animals,
shut away in their cages.

In your dreams
I wonder if you think you are like them?
If when you wake in the cold of the night,
unable to move yourself,
you feel weak. Vulnerable.
If only we could explain to each other, if I
could show
you
how I feel, and you could show me too.
Divided then through our quiet bitterness.
My strength I inherited from you, my
hate
of your wastage; your
misery
of not seeing me complete the walkway,
to make the connection with adulthood.
We are alike in our weakness against the wind,

but together our
strength
lives.
At a time of fading, you are the body. Your mind
thinks now
but its strength is still ignited through us.

In the dead of night your dreams are real,
your clammy white legs are unable to breath their
own
release.
You can't even hold yourself for protection.
I curl myself into a ball and hug myself
withdrawn into myself.
We both do in a way.
But you can't hug yourself, so I must hug you.
Even though I don't, my arms surround you.
I try to protect you,
the wind can blow me over
and its noise can ring in my ears, as I sit in my little
ball.
You are the adult I will become, my respect
has never wavered.

Our togetherness shines and people comment
on our connection. No visible lines connect us,
our experiences are different but we share this

pain.
We are the same.
Father and daughter.
I love you, and say it in verse and you love me too. I
know.
If only we were open enough to see our division.

Our quietness is echoed
by the loss of

Words. Words. Words.

Rebecca Westwood
Stamford Poet Laureate 2015 - 16

THE SPANISH STEPS

I wanted to sit on the Spanish steps
to write a poem
next to the house in which Keats' life ended.

At twenty five years old

the eternal poet.

The memorial on the wall read 'The English Poet'.
What a wonderful title to have.

The sun lit its flickering flame upon the steps

making it hard to see the mix of fashion
sounds of language,
families, couples
puffer jackets,
merging
modernity on the steps of history.

Stone carved out into the distance
domes, gargoyles
television aerials.
Green shutters against yellow buildings.

Dressed up gladiators
wanting money for photographs.

I wanted to see the Trevi fountain
to capture its white majesty on my page.

Instead
as the sun dropped behind the houses
my feet wrapped up in plasters

I sat on some comfy steps
by a military house
nestled
into the last of the sunshine,

my boy beside me
on our first anniversary.

Tired, blistered,
satiated by high tea and champagne
holding onto a moment
in words.

An English poet
in an Italian world.

Rebecca Westwood
Stamford Poet Laureate 2015 - 16

STAMFORD STONES

Sunlight falls on town stones
Glowing – glinting beneath the beam
Centuries church spires pierce sky
Lost castle solid against storm
River reflects back beneath swans
Fish-scales shimmer between reeds
Now, as for Bladud's Athenian philosophers
Or Oxford scholars later

In some courts, alleys and passages
Shadows never shift from corners
Down dark steps – between buildings
Splinters of night linger
Fallen from mail coaches
Or Rose War warriors

Cardinal Cox

SIR ROBERT'S TOMB, ST. MARY'S STAMFORD

(After William Morris)

Here lies noble Sir Robert of this town
He was brave and the Easterlings did fight
Here too we did then fair Ellayne lie down.
He was known as a good Christian knight
She did wait while he fought in foreign wars
And won back his heart when he did return,
For but few short days widows gown she wore.
Of her wrath another maid did once learn
Across the river does her rival lie
For spurned she did quickly sicken and fade
Robert did not notice when she did die
Buried without memorial that maid.
All three mortals now are in the cold earth
Think on this fate for all who suffer birth.

Cardinal Cox

WILLIAM STUKELEY

Reading Cesar's War and surveying stones
From apothecary he learnt herb lore
Wondered what the mossy menhir was for
And watches workmen bring up old bones

London, initiated a mason
Once halting a sermon to watch eclipse
Pondering on St. John's Apocalypse
Drops black ink into a midnight basin

Dubs princess as Archdruidess of Kew
Her crown of mistletoe, ivy and oak
Observes the geese skein with a fenman's eye
Knows them migrating to edge of the sky
Searches for the lost knowledge of the folk
Remembers fields where heard the cuckoo

Cardinal Cox

ROBERT OWEN

We should not worship gods that look to chide
Or those small deities that crave our praise
Who consign innocents to sacred blaze
Sitting in judgement on those who have died

Let us live our lives without their fury
Let young learn in play with what attracts them
Factories enough await to condemn
Without spirits acting as a jury

The poor can be helped into better lives
Communities of equals we've to build
For we're all members of the human race

It is not enough for them to survive
Homes to be constructed, fields to be tilled
Healthy, well fed, a future they can face

Cardinal Cox

WHEN TIME RUNS OUT
(THE REALISATION)

When time runs out,
There's one last breath
As a million young men
Face their death;
One million sigh
With firm intent,
One choir of collective
Stern lament:
"What twist of fate
Has brought us here?,
To grasp this stomach churning fear,
to fight the evil cause of those
Who have no god above themselves?
"These thoughts now echo through the minds
Of a million faces now resigned;
each Khaki shoulder bound together,
To shield some Generals unmarked leather;
Small crosses held,
Last letters read,
Hope discharged while
Prayers are pledged.
As time runs out
The tears are shed,
As two million boots
Step to the edge.
An hour of weight,
While seconds pass,

Then comes that
Searing whistle blast;
One million hearts
Now beating fast,
In a race to see
Who's beating last?
When gunfire drowns
One final shout
"My fate be with us!!!...

...When time runs out.

John Learoyd

THE STANDER

Silhouette on wet cobblestones, motionless mourner,
Solitary sinner with nothing inside.
The Turner brushed burning sky lights up the stander,
Revealing the horror he's struggling to hide.
Firemen try vainly to beckon him back,
From the bricks and the glass, as they crash to his feet;
But he does not respond to these heroes in ruins
Unravelling their hoses on Copperfield street;
His half hunter chimes to remind him he's living,
It's trying to give him a reason to leave,
But his conscience ignores the alarm in his pocket
For, he's trapped in his locket of pure disbelief.
Two sons and a wife had cried for him loudly,
As Berlin's dark messengers blackened their sky;
They'd screamed out his name as he ran to This horror,
But screams would not alter the way they would die.
His fear had not faltered the fury above them,
His home was engulfed by these devils from hell;
The shock from each blast would disfigure the skyline,
Freezing his body, destroying his soul.

The firemen extinguished the flames of his life,
Two sons and a wife, three innocent dead,
Yet this was a copy of the carnage delivered
When he'd given the orders to the men he had led.
Men who had said they would follow him gladly,
Acknowledged his rank as they boarded his plane;

They flew out to targets hidden in darkness,
One single intent, to cause damage and pain;

The grey bay doors opened, their payload was dropped
On that night, their incendiaries tore a city apart,
Now the fate of his victims scarred the ruins before him,
Forever engraved on the walls of his heart.

Silhouette on wet cobblestones,
A motionless mourner, solitary sinner
With nowhere to hide, his cries for his family
And for those he has slaughtered
Are being echoed by Standers on the opposite side

John Learoyd

NOT EVERY SOLDIER (THE REALITY)

Not every soldier is serving his country,
Not every soldier swears an oath to his queen.
Not every soldier is a fully trained fighter.
Who follows convention, claims he's morally clean.
Not every soldier agrees with the advert
"be a part of the team, be part of the best,"
Not every soldier will conform to his orders
Thank f*** there are soldiers not afraid to protest.
Not every soldier is a gifted tactician
Who can plan in advance for misfortunes to come,
And not every soldier can keep cool in the crisis,
Has respect for his buddy or faith in the gun
Not every soldier wants to peace-keep the planet?
Predicting the outcomes, finding reasons for war
And how many soldiers crave an enemies terror?,
Its not every soldier who wants this pain to endure.
And does every soldier want a posthumous medal?
Given the choice would he pray for his life?
Because not every soldier wants his flag covered coffin
Paraded through Wiltshire In front of his wife
Not every soldier who loses a limb
Wants help for a hero or your false sympathy,
Some of these soldiers may acknowledge their
nightmares
Yet too many suffer from P.T.S.D.
Not every soldier can become a civilian
Not every civvie knows a serviceman's pride

Few understand what some soldiers have been through
The trauma that drives some to commit suicide.
Not every soldier will agree with this poem,
The lines are not written to **dispel** all they loose
For many are braver than the guy who is writing
and they've gained the right to think as they choose,
but
Not every soldier from the ranks that I served in
Could see through the bullshit and political lies
There were so many youngsters who believed in
excitement
Yet had not the courage to stop and ask...

...Why.

John Learoyd

AMORAL STORY

(After watching the BBC's 'Frozen Planet')

Guillemot chick, uncertain on the ledge,
the distant shining sea seems out of reach.
Its anxious parents coax it to the edge,
and urge it to the surf, beyond the beach.

With sudden whirring wings the chick takes flight
from off the cliff, goes speeding through the air;
desperate, vainly straining to keep height,
till crashing on the sand in mute despair.

Sickening impact, stupefying bounce,
yet still the fledgling tries to stagger on.
A patient arctic fox, with lightning pounce,
snatches the stricken bird, turns, and is gone.

Impassive Nature sifts the weak from strong.
It's live or die and never right or wrong.

Phil Dunkerley

THE MAN OF TRUST

He came in trust, they called him 'Father'; he
was reverenced for his intellect and preaching.
As local envoy of the Holy See,
he meekly followed Rome and all its teaching.

His moral precepts were their guide and stay,
and he eschewed each carnal urge and snare.
He always walked the straight and narrow way,
and little children were his special care.

For twenty years he touched the children's hearts,
inducing them to bare their souls and all.
For twenty years he touched their private parts,
and threatened them to keep them in his thrall.

O hypocrite! You know, and know damn well,
if it exists, you'll be consigned to Hell!

Phil Dunkerley

David,
Dear Friend
Best Wishes
Phil.

NAME AND NUMBER

When self-awareness first arose in man
he also recognised the self in others,
and to identify them he began
to give to each a name, as friends and brothers.
And then about six hundred years ago,
because two people often shared one name,
a second epithet was used, to show
that John Smith and John Jones were not the same.

But nowadays our names do not suffice
and we are strings of digits in computers.
Perhaps such systems may be more precise,
but many of us feel they do not suit us.

Trapped deep in cyberspace and databases,
we hanker still for friendly names and faces.

Phil Dunkerley

LICHENS

The short sad days of winter hurt my mind;
a stultifying greyness, cold and drear,
pervades the world; no joy in it I find,
and everything's withdrawn and life austere.

Then one day, un-forewarned, the dawn breaks clear,
the sun pours out a cold and brittle light.
I walk the fields, I feel a rising cheer,
the sky is blue, the air is pure and bright.

O precious day, a boon from season's spite,
too early for the trees to bud again!
But look! A living green and gold delight
my eye on branch and bole in vivid stain.

So from the bitter depth of winter strife
the silent lichens nurse the spring to life.

Phil Dunkerley

THEY ALL GO TO M & S

Back in the day the politicians,
used to take a strong position.
It may have been a sixty nine,
or wife swaps at a cheese and wine.
Today they hang on to their keys,
scared of birds and scared of bees.
Stripped bare of any sex appeal,
there's nothing that they need conceal.
Expenses crises? Dull I tell ya.
Can't you bring back David Mellor?

Long ago they had wild stories,
we used to know what made them Tories.
From left to right now it's the same,
intent on dishing out the blame.
They point bent fingers, tell white lies,
whilst sporting (sweet!) each other's ties.
Tories in red, Labour in blue,
a mixed-up, muddy pot of stew.

It used to be all S and M,
not so now, it's just not them.
It's all turned round (let's thank the press),
they all now go to M and S.

Camilla McLean

THE SAN ANTONIO SONNET

This party town's aflame with booze tonight,
And through the drunken streets I drift alone,
The stags and hens may clash and start their fights,
But not with me, my ghost floats on unknown,

I wonder what they feel, are they aware?
Oblivious, they drink, he shouts, she cries,
I wander lost but curious I stare,
Observing my own kin with sober eyes.

But some of me would like a part in this:
This wall of noise, these lanes that smell of chips.
They're happy here, they have their place, their bliss,
These northern lassies shaking pie-fed hips.

I don't belong here, don't belong to you.
I'm neither here nor there, that's nothing new.

Camilla McLean

XYZ

X and I thought we were the perfect combination.
I didn't know he was X at the time,
we thought we'd be together infinitely.

In mathematics, X is commonly used as the name
for an independent variable
or unknown value.
An independent variable you certainly were
but not so much as I.
Silly I.
I didn't appreciate your unknown value.
And now, though you're X,
I can be very proud to have been Mrs X.

And still might still have been if Y hadn't entered
the equation.
Y oh Y.
Silly I.
Y marched in and I sighed,
X + Y + I equals...
Well, it does not add up.
X was subtracted and then...
I would like to say as little as possible about Y.
Looking back, Y is all there is to say.

Then I was all alone,
regretting the problems I had caused.

But then, though I wasn't looking for Z,
and Z wasn't looking for I.
It turned out the be the magic combination.
I can say that maths has never been a strong point,
but with Z it all adds up perfectly.
Z is where is all ends.
And if I'm lucky, Z brings me a cup of tea in bed.

Camilla McLean

MUSINGS ON WEE

(after To a Mouse by Robert Burns)

Now, if you're anything at all like me,
You're a bit of a fan of the wee word 'wee'
(that's the one with a double 'ee').
You see?
Not the one with two silly 'i's,
Despite its apparently appropriate size.
The wee that we (one 'e') are talking aboot,
Has something of a Scottish root.
It's not that wee that smells of pee.
Nor Japanese Nintendo Wii,
I guarantee.
When Mr. Burns addressed his creature,
He meant that tiny was his feature.

Camilla McLean

STAGEFRIGHT

Life's a comedy. Breathless in the wings.
I wait the cue you never think to give.
Limelight tugs my heart, footlights raise my hopes.
But, sickened with first night nerves, I freeze.

I should be bold, dismiss all doubts, and strut
Confident, masterful, across the boards.
I've learnt the script – rehearsed lines in my head
a thousand times – yet tongue-tied, flounder on.

Scenery weaves its spell across the stalls.
From the wings its transient nature's plain.
Greasepaint conceals my star struck walk-on part.
A tattered threadbare costume does for me.

Night's candles shine on Juliet. I stand
backstage, for me no Romeo's entrance.
Spear carrier, I shuffle on, ignored.
Upstaged among your entourage I lurk.

The play's the thing but yet I fear to act.
The motley's on – the pensive audience waits.
The bouquets come, the critics sing your praise.
You take applause; no encores called for me.

No happy endings close this scene. At fall
Of curtain, my tragedy turns to farce.

They'll hear no punchline to this jester's joke.
I'm speechless – prompt me, for I dry.

Richard Barter

THREADING THE NEEDLE

Her petulant frown, her irate mumble
and I see my younger self.
I was four, or maybe five
and the needle's gaping hole
refused to take the thread.

I sucked the end and poked.
It curled and twisted.
Scowling in frustration,
I stamped infuriated feet.
Again I tried
but never would it go.

Her hand enclosed mine.
The tip crept forward.
Not snagging in that annoying way,
it lipped trough releasing me to sew
and stitch, in time embroider.

Her touch not always welcome
-a mother's cautions rankle
however sage the words –
her shaking head, her "I told you so's"
as galling as recalcitrant thread.

Now she needs my touch
and I must remember

to stifle impatience
... and smile ... and joke.

No footsteps announce
her coming.
She knocks on no door,
rings no bell.

Creeping unnoticed
she hovers at your shoulder.
Her sighs brush your cheek.

One morning you'll awake
to find her
patient at your bedside.

Silent sands trickle
till all that's left
is to count the days
and wonder how
they've fled.

Richard Barter

MATING GAME

She spies him, motionless in the grass,
flirts and runs away.
Others watch,
tired of her indifference.
He lopes behind knowing she'll wait.
Toying with a length of vetch
she senses his approach.
He comes too close – touches.
She whirls, talon long, strong legs.
Fists brush his dodging cheek,
sing past his ducking ear.
Half hearted jabs fend off her blows.
His flurry of punches stab the air.

Rough and playful wins the day.
She turns her back, lies still,
pretends to nibble a blade of grass.

Then up he leaps,
memories of prowess fading,
and off he runs to seek another.
She lies unmoved,
memory stretching
to the future.
A few weeks content
and then the urgent
hiding of her young

dotted in forms about the field;
visited at dawn, at dusk,
until hawk spots one,
fox steals second.
With luck two survive
-a doe to play coquette,
a buck to woo.

Richard Barter

PENELOPE

During the night the needlewoman came.
Stealthily unpicking late Summer greens
she threaded in October's golds and reds.

Her tapestry of hillsides and hedgerows,
fields and trees she wove afresh with colours
glorying under the western sinking sun.

On lonely footpaths, among bleak copses
drift leaves curling and wilting into death,
like confetti from forgotten weddings.

Secretly she came, unstitching in the dark
his burial shroud, leaving branches bare
and gaunt, sombre against a pearl grey sky.

Soon Winter's slender skeins will make their mark
and icy frosts fold frozen traceries
on black fingers which stroke the pale moon's face.

Faithful, over her vibrant silks she waits.
Needles laden with sharp and startling hues
lie ready, impatient in their basket.

While snows yet melt on distant hills, and winds
moan sadly from the north, she'll summon forth
her threads and weave anew Spring's fresher greens...

… and stitch new buds and bursting open leaves,
yellow aconite and daring primrose,
snowdrop's nodding head and white hellebore.

Then reaching up to welcome sunlight's rays
and greet Odysseus come newly home –
a dash of blue on woodland's murky floor.

Richard Barter

FAIR ENOUGH

Beware the Ides of March, they say,
For the Fair is surely on its way
The largest of its kind in Lincolnshire
Once referenced by William Shakespeare
Amid Henry IV's historic pages
But it's changed a lot since the Middle Ages
Our town's endured a thousand years
Of this fest of blood and sweat and tears

Steam-powered roundabouts and elephant parades
Have given way to the escapades
Of underaged hooligans and louts
Issuing foolish whoops and shouts
As their parents' money is so carelessly frittered
Away, and soon the streets are littered
With wrappers and cans and the odd smashed bottle
When rambunctiousness reaches full throttle
And they're even less likely to repent
At this pious time of year, mid lent

The tell-tale signs that this time's approaching
Occur when convoys of lorries start encroaching
On our roads, holding up the traffic
Painted to appeal to their key demographic
With lurid murals that vaguely resemble
Cartoons and celebrities, then men hastily assemble
Their ramshackle rides, the ferris wheels

And roller coasters, and begin their spiels
As you stroll up, ‘roll up and hand over your cash
Hop aboard and hope we don’t crash.’

It’s begun, so I must run for shelter
From kids belting down the helter skelter
Many a hand still bears the scars
Of drink driving on the bumper cars
Dodging the flying nuts and bolts
From the waltzer screeching to a halt
The brakes on these things are bound to be faulty
And all the food tastes too sweet or too salty
What dogs did they put in these soggy hot dogs?
But the kids don’t care, their eyes agog
Peering through the fog of candy floss
Dad suffers a loss on the impossible ring toss
And you know he’s really out of luck
When he fails to hook a single duck
And the children can’t tear their teary eyes
Away from each unreachable oversized prize

I received an anonymous tip off
The whole affair’s synonymous with ‘rip off’
I can afford to show no lenience
To this major inconvenience
I’m growing increasingly annoyed
With this so-called fun you just can’t avoid

My eyes are sore from the piercing lasers
That tear through the sky like giant razors
Through paper, you can't escape the beat
Of the top forty hits on infinite repeat
I can't stand to hear another club anthem
But at least at last it's gone off to Grantham.

Joe Hoten

LEAST FUN ON THE HILL

It's 8 o'clock on a winter's morning
And I see why there was a weather warning
Flakes are falling all around
And fade into the featureless ground
But duty calls so I must forgo
The lie in, and wade through all this snow
It's too unsafe to ride a bicycle
Plus now, mine more resembles an icicle
I don two jackets, a coat and two scarves
No point doing these things by halves

After one more coffee, I can delay no more
I leave the warmth, and step through the door
Tightly clutching the key in my pocket
And hoping this time I remembered to lock it
It's all too easy to forsake
Such things when you're only half awake
But I've come too far, I've sealed my fate
If I run back and check, I'll be too late
It's simply not within my power
To run this way then that within an hour
I have no choice but to resign
Myself to the daily dreary decline

It's difficult for me not to begrudge
Each car that drives past as I trudge
Along, sneezing, trying not to freeze,
Fighting against the biting breeze
My coat's lost a button, I've broken the zip

And across the frost I stumble and slip.

My stinging eyes can barely perceive
The path, strewn as it is with leaves,
Branches, twigs and other detritus
I'm sure this cold's becoming bronchitis

I'm woeful as Wothorpe Nursery nears
Stamford's about a mile from here
There's a thorn in my side and now through my sole
As it stabs through my shoe and leaves a hole
Now each cautious step causes searing pain
To course through my body and rattle my brain
It was foolish of me to even attempt
To rely on a route so unclear and unkempt.

I'm praying now that some friend of mine
Will drive up beside me, as if by design
They'd lean across and, smiling, say:
'I drive past you nearly every day
Aren't you tired of walking this far?'
I'd shrug 'I don't really need a car.
Just doing my bit to save the planet.
Yours coughs out monoxide, someone should ban it.'

But on this coldest of days, I have no such luck
Instead, I get splashed by a Morrisons truck
My legs are soaking, and I have a hunch
That was no twig I just heard crunch

I'm plodding along in jeans most sodden
Not stopping to see on what I've trodden
Old beers cans and broken glass
Cast asunder under the overpass
I try not to picture the dying squeal
Of each snail crushed by my clumsy heel.
Other roadside casualties are more unpleasant
A badger, a rabbit and half a pheasant
I doubt a single one of them reckoned
If they crossed the road, they'd be dead in a second

I begin to doubt I have the strength
To continue, but, indeed, at length
Stamford begins to emerge from the murk
I made it, and my reward is going to work
But the end of the day is even worse
As I must repeat this ordeal in reverse
I'm not certain I can even cope
With the killer 4 kilometre slope
I don't understand, and perhaps never will,
Why they built Easton on a bloody hill.

Joe Hoten

ODE TO AMETHYST

O lavender stone with deep purple hues:
Ten million years, then: no longer hidden from view:
Concealed inside unassuming rocks
Iron, water and sand they trickled amok.
The shape of your crystal on an atomic scale
A pyramid forms, yet your colours prevail:
So now we bow down to your regal-ness clear
and wear you with pride in our jewellery all year
Yet -

Before:
The power you had over Bacchus himself -
The wearers they knew the secret you held.
It follows you still, eons later you see:
you give us Protection for us to be free.
Your lavender core in a mauve spangled dust -
Angels they too see the strength in this trust -
We humans not perfect as crystals so pure
Can stop the attraction of your colours' allure

O lavender beauty, O February stone:
As pale as a pastel, as royal as a throne
You transcend us all, you've existed forever
You're our link with the past:
Amethyst, Our treasure.

Wendy McLean

I KNOW ABOUT YOU

I know about the empty seat on the bus,
next to me, all the way on the journey into town.
I know you would rather stand in the bus,
in the aisle, getting jerked by the brakes and not fall down.
I know the sick feeling that I get
When I move my bag to make space on the left -
You do not respond.
You would rather stand.
You would rather stand in the bus
that is full with one empty seat – so clearly in view -
But: I know about you.
You're a woman, with a bag, on the bus
into town, leaving me nonplussed:
We might browse the same shops, and touch the same scarves,
We'll drink Earl Grey tea, and eat our scones in halves,
We'll even watch the same movie scenes
and enjoy the same fantastic dreams -
But: I know about you.
You speak volumes when you shun my act
when you see me move my bag to my lap
to make space for you.
I know what you really are. I know.
Is it my uncertain heritage?
Is the clue in my choice of beverage?

Is it my curly hair or my darker skin?
Or is it that I'm not too thin?
I watch the world through knowing eyes
I watch window seats get occupied
I watch the aisle seats get full,
but mine remains empty still.
I know my seat's the last vacant one,
- Sometimes it gets a thankful bum-
You are often there at the time,
But you'll not take the seat right next to mine.
You'll not sit beside one so different from you
Yet underneath we could share the same allure.
I shrug yet again - I've stopped rolling my eyes -
The irony of Freedom: keeps telling me lies:
That Racism lives alive and well
in a country that claims to have banished the bells
and shackles from other-coloured skins.
But the way that you are, your reception stings
a pang shoots through me - the hurt it brings .
I can't stop the knock, or stop the pain
That rips blood red into my veins -
- we're all red underneath at the start.
Melanin molecules covering our blood
bring out the worst in our prejudiced hearts.
It's just a journey on a bus into town
You'll avoid the space and not even frown -
I know it'll be the same.

You will pretend that all is well
– I bitterly hope your leg veins swell -
It's hard on your knees when you stand on your feet -
Try to balance yourself as the bus stops with a screech.
I know what you're like, I know your real worth
is less than a penny, no, much less than a squirt
I know about you, white whimpish woman you are:
I know.
I know about you.

Wendy McLean

LIBERTY, EQUALITY, FRATERNITY
HOW SOON IT MAY BE GONE

How soon before our Freedom to talk openly
will be taken away?
How soon before we can't express
our inner thoughts as we may?
How soon before our cries of anguish
will be crushed
By Powers that be when freedom of speech
is turned right into mush?
Should citizens be more careful
to shout out their objections ?
Should we fear to be accused
of subversive political intentions?
I worry that this Old World,
that declared itself as Free,
Will remove all liberties, all human rights,
from both you and me.
So many of us enjoy a thriving Capitalist life –
if it's money you have, you'll have no hunger
and no strife.
There has always been the fear,
of the laws of the land;
Many who have spoken up, and vented their
thoughts were grand.
But many more have never really been that bold
For fear of recrimination, or so I have been told.
So why am I venting my anger over here?
Is my own life in danger, should I live in fear?

If the police suspect or just think I have a plot
I can be shot dead on sight, whether I do or not.
Is this what we want,
in a place formerly with many freedoms?
Is this how we must live to justify
our leaders' terrorisms?
How long will this last? What Wrongs can we face?
Should we all join the Armed forces,
you know, just in case -
In case we need to have the power, be the guilty one
who makes that grave decision,
through the barrel of a gun?
Who will decide to shoot down a poet
with biting words
With words that are quite powerful,
or words that are absurd?
It's all put in perspective,
when I worry about my Liberty
Should not all of us be worried?
What about Fraternity?
I mourn the slain
of all the many recent global murders
I mourn sadly too now more countries
will close their borders
I mourn for loss of innocence and loss of privacy
I mourn that after all that work,
we'll also lose Equality

There is almost no point to openly mourn
the ones killed by flash flooding
Caused by global climate change –
another human bidding –
But sadly these deaths are not affected
my grand Libertarian rant
And am I being a little selfish
to worry I'll not be able to chant?
The anger of the terrors that Terror begets itself
Doesn't justify more Terror
into which we're all engulfed
We can mourn the murdered dead,
but a gun may still point at our heads:
Liberty, Equality and Fraternity – we need them:
The way things are going,
might still be Death to our Total Freedom.

Wendy McLean

CREDO (OR STUPIDITY)

As a child, I believed
For every drop of rain that fell a flower grew
For every kind word my mummy said
a lesson was learnt
That each new day that dawned on earth
progress was made.

As a young man, I believed
For every pound I paid in tax a child was fed
For every vote I cast in earnest society progressed
That every day I toiled away created happiness and
wealth

Now in my dotage I still believe
For every banker the taxpayer pays
a hundred jobs are saved
That every time the central bank prints money
wealth is created
For every politician who opens his mouth
much happiness will follow.

Chin Tan

LA VIEILLE DAME SANS CERVEAU

O what can ail thee, economy
So sick and palely loitering
The yield has withered from the gilts
And markets sink

O what can ail thee, economy
So indebted and so cash begone
The bankers' granaries are full
And the harm is done.

I see a green shoot on thy chart
With weakly stem and good signs few
And confidence's a fading trend
Fast withereth too

I met a banker in the flesh
Full beautiful his bespoke suit
His face was long his fingers light
And his eyes were wild

For the spied the granny of Threadneedle street
In London town, a fragrant zone
He looked at her as he did love
And made sweet moan

He set her on his derivative
She nothing else saw all day long

For sideways would she bend and yield
The nation's gold

She gave him cash fresh off the press
Low interest rates and regulations few
And sure in language strange she said
I love thee true.

He took her to his trading floor
And there he wept and sighed full sore
O'er his balance sheet so broke and poor
With figures false

And there he lulled her asleep
And there she believed –Ah woe betide-
The strangest tale he ever told
On the need for QE

I saw pale interns, and unpaid too;
Pale taxpayers, unwashed and all
They cried: finance is a parasite
It sucks society bone dry

I saw their starved lips in the gloam
With horrid warning gaped wide
And I could not wake as from a dream
For it was real

And that is why I sojourn here
So sick and palely loitering
As yield is withering from the gilts
And markets sink.

Chin Tan

LIBERTY

Liberty, we love liberty
The very word melts the hardest hearts
Radiates a warm glow that lasts
Till the next sound bite
We congratulate ourselves on our noble nature
Even as the urge for liberty
Drive reasonable men to march in columns
To go kill some mother's son abroad.

We forget we are sheep
Sniffing the air to discern the temper of the flock
Mimicking the antics of celebrities
Sucking at the udder of populist ideas
Fawning at the foot of political correctness
Scoffing at the thoughtful few who dare
Say things that do not soothe the common ear.

Give us Big Government for we need
To protect our Liberty with regulations
Armed police, laws, prisons and bailiffs
Of which we have many more
Than ol King John's clerks and sheriffs
And his one sad Magna Parchment.

Many are the benefits of Big Government:
The Serious Fraud Office protects us from bankers
The Met protects us from conservative party whips

The Central Bank protects us from rising house prices
The Food Standards Agency protects us from horsemeat
The Environmental Agency gives us sandbags when it rains

And when the shit hits the fan,
Let's have an official inquiry, a new quango
To whitewash the mess, and dilute the blame
For this is democracy, transparency, accountability
And too bad nobody is to blame
We'll do better next time
And try not to be caught.

Thus are we well protected
From unpasteurised milk
From the need to make any effort
From the tedium of figuring things out
From the responsibility of our actions
From the solitude of serious thought.

Chin Tan

GRAMMAR

I am brave, you are courageous, he is foolhardy
I am determined, you are firm, he is obstinate
I am interesting, you are eccentric, he is nuts
I am wise, you are knowledgeable,
he is jack of all trades
I communicate, you disseminate, he gossips
I invent, you improvise, he muddles through
I invest, you acquire, he spends
I weigh, you ponder, he dithers,
I dance, you waltz, he prances
I orate, you speak, he chatters
I sing, you hum, he croaks
I write poetry, you versify, he scribbles
I have faith, you are religious, he is fundamentalist
I sip, you drink, he sucks
I taste, you eat, he gobbles
I spend a penny, you wash your hands, he pisses
My dog did it, you have wind, he farts.

Chin Tan

PATRON

Art is
cloistered
collages
framed
in red velvet
in wine glasses
an in-joke
in stiff smiles
counting splashes

a foreigner
on clean walls
of menace
in white
curtains
champagne
a conversation
green baize
with dice

Graffiti is
street theatre
a broken window
with the latest gig

a lingering murder
on brick
papered
a postcard

The word is
spilt ink
swallowing
a foolishness

a cv on an envelope
colour of shards
cleverness
for longevity

Mike Alderson

WALKING BACKWARDS

A man is walking backwards
                    into the future
seeing solidity
      in the movement of waves
          a structure of atoms
        a place   a time
a perception

a man is walking backwards
          and his future is certain
he gets up from his desk
    walks through the sand
  and
          wherever it is
                was certain

he looks at each frame
            as it hardens into history
  nothing moves in it
                          he does not choose
  but
              walks backwards
                          into his future

Mike Alderson

STANLEY

It's a bulldog of sorts, standing
disregarded in the pub,
loneliness in both poise and posture.

His head moves, his master's voice
somewhere and waiting
he rests his chin on a chair.

Those eyes have a look of years.
His interest wanes as I finish
The rustle and smell of peanuts.

Proximity is unsettling,
Unfamiliarity breeds fear, reputations.
He seems to know and moves away

Mike Alderson

READING TIME

Here I whittle time, like aa dry stick
(Douglas Dunn – St Kilda's Parliament)

in a second hand copy
from the Heart Foundation
she writes at the end of the line
in the cluttered white space
she has assigned for notes
nothing to do
as if taking time is empty
written off

a lack of action indicates
wasted seas
deserted rocks
burnt flotsam
as if quiet thoughts are wasted
thc pursuit of happiness
reduced to filling slots of time
an inventory of chatter

I steal such moments to whittle time
and in my moments
I am again outside the abacus.

Mike Alderson

THE DEATH OF DANIEL LAMBERT AGED 39

The crowds dwindle down and eventually number
but a few,
The few finally become one, this remaining witness
tires of my lack of activity and leaves the now
darkening room.
I shift my body and, as the candlelight breaks free of
the contours of my frame, it reveals the nakedness of
the room:
A chair, a table and a heat-less fire, its childish
immature flames dancing on the embers

I go to move, to reach to for the fire, not for the
heat, but to create some noise.
A crackle at least, please, to drown out the wheezing
of my chest,
But as I reach out, the shackles of my weight pull me
squarely back into the chair, slumped
Defeated
Cheated
Again

The polite lady has now entered the room, her feet
more softly spoken than her as she passes to the
table and leaves me some food
Some food, more food
Food: the making of me,
Food: the death of me.

She goes to say something, but notices the fire,
Distracted she stabs with a poker at the juvenile
flames, they avoid her glances and spit sparks at her
feet, fueled with a new spirit they rise up and she
backs off, retreating from the room

I curse the flames for their antics
I curse the food for my size
I curse myself for this life

I relish the day when the numbers dwindle to nil
When the only visitors are my friends not these idle
bored minds seeking a visual fix
They mock and they taunt, begging me to eat
Not knowing. No. Knowing, but not caring that I
can't take much more

I wish for the day when I can walk again, to move
unseen, unheard, pass between crowds rather than
stop them and cause traffic

My heart is now heavy, laden with fat and strains
somewhere deep inside,
Each breath in is an effort to lift my chest, but
followed with the relief of an exhale as my body
returns to its sunken state
Shorter breaths in, harder to rise

Deeper breaths out, slumping further into the chair
Shorter still, no longer rising, just falling further,
further down.
From the chair I slip to the ground, exhaling the
whole way.
There's no other noise,
just the sigh as I'm laid across the stone floor
My head sinks back and the timbers above me
slowly flicker out of sight

I stand up and peel myself away from this aged
burden of fat and bones
Head west across the meadows, following the
Welland back towards Leicestershire
To the fields of my dreams,
Where my youthful self ran
And played and hunted and smiled
And smiled
Following the river, I chase the memories of those
smiles.

Jimmy Pea

CURIOSITY KILLED THE CAT

Curiosity killed the cat,
Desperation destroyed the dog,
The elephant's expiration
was explained by exhaustion
And fame finished the fox.

Greed got to the giraffe,
Hunger hindered the horse,
An infectious inquisition inhibited the iguana
And jealousy jostled the jellyfish.

Knowledge knackered the kangaroo,
Laziness limited the lizard,
The mouse was mutilated by a meticulous manner
And naughtiness nailed the nag.
Opulence obliterated the owl,
Politeness prohibited the parrot,
The quail was quashed by a quantity of questions
And revenge ravished the rat.
Selfishness starved the stoat,
Tiredness terminated the tiger,
The urchin was undone by an unfounded
understanding
And variety vanquished the vole.
Worry wiped out the walrus,
Extremities exterminated the Xantus,
The yak was yielded by a youthful yearning
And zealousness zapped the zebra.

Admiration abolished the alligator,
Bravery butchered the bison,
Can we really be sure that all these crimes went unreported.

And that curiosity killed the cat?

Jimmy Pea

OWL-ME

My follow up to The Owl and The Pussycat

The owl had the pussy-cat up in a tree
On a beautiful summer's night,
She screamed and she cried,
she thought she had died
But lacked the strength for a fight.
She fell to the earth and later gave birth,
To a thing that made her quite ill.
To the Owl she said, I wish I was dead,
I thought I had taken the pill,
The pill,
The pill,
I thought I had taken the pill!

Owl said to his offspring, 'You horrible thing!
How ugly and evil you look!
You purr like a cat, but fly like a bat
And your beak it resembles a hook.'
So Owl hid it away, for two years and a day,
But soon it flew up to the skies.
Owl took out his gun, aimed at his son
And shot it between its two eyes,
Two eyes,
Two eyes,
And shot it between its two eyes.

Without his young head, soon Owl's offspring was dead
And his corpse slumped down to the ground.
His father lacked doubt, as the blood spewed out,
That his son's body would never be found.
So they dug a small hole, behind a grassy knoll
And believed they had hidden their sin.
But there in the wood a Piggy-wig stood
And took photos of them killing their kin
Their kin,
Their kin,
And took photos of them killing their kin.

Piggy went to the Police, to report the decease
Of the weird thing he'd seen fall from the sky.
They arrested the owl, charged with murder most fowl
And the judge told the Owl he would die.
But Owl's case went to appeal and he managed a deal
That involved him blaming the Cat
The Cat let out a howl, sprang at the Owl
And the judge donned his little black hat
Black hat,
Black hat,
And the judge donned his little black hat.

The Owl and the Pussy Cat went to jail
In a pitiful horse drawn cart.
They took no money, were starved of honey

And jail did drive them apart.
Owl took his own life, with a blunt wooden knife
And Pussy Cat's death came all too soon.
So, side by side, the Owl and his bride
Were buried by the light of the moon,
The moon,
The moon,
Were buried by the light of the moon.

Jimmy Pea

CURB SCRAWLIN'

Don't cry over spilt milk
Unless the milk is yellow
And has the properties of paint
And is spilt over a cobbled street
That has been here for hundreds of years,
In which case, cry some more!

But your tears won't wash away those lines,
You'll need a pressure washer for that
And two days to spare
And three men whilst you're at it
One to point,
One to scrub,
And one to keep the numbers up.

The lines were yellow,
The residents saw red,
The council felt blue
And like the freshly elected lines
They cracked under a bit of pressure.

The lines have now gone,
but the council is still here.
Is it time to curb their spending?
After all, these streets aren't paved with gold
Just gilded around the curbs.

Jimmy Pea

WHAT IS THE POINT IN A WASP?

There's one thing in a wasp that you should try to avoid.
It's that thing with a sting tucked neatly inside.
Many things rhyme with buzz, bee and honey.
But try a rhyme for wasp – now that's not a bit funny.
A wasp will not pollinate because that's not its thing.
At one end twitchy whiskers, at the other a sting.
If you swat a wasp it'll get you, eventually.
And sting you several times.
It's just once with a bee.
There seems neither rhyme nor reason
Why wasps have a season.
The point in a wasp
Still eludes me.

Andrew Croft

MAN FLU

It started with a sniffle,
Followed by a sneeze or two.
But within a matter of hours
I came down with man flu.

First I put on a brave face,
But when you have got man flu
It's impossible to smile.
It always gets the better of you.

Straight upstairs to bed I go,
Tissues, tablets – any will do.
It's a terrible thing to have, you know?
And it's sure to last a week or two.

I'll lie and laze about all day,
But a woman's cold soon goes away.
What on earth am I going to do?
It is so hard to have this thing, man flu.

I'll deserve an Oscar, and that's a fact
My dying swan's a fine old act!
"You poor fragile thing you
Suffering with the man flu."

At this rate, recovery looks bleak.
And yet I know I'll struggle through.

We are now thinking well into the third week.
Even plagued as we are with this man flu.

I just asked my wife if a cure she knew.
But she replied – as ladies always do.

“Come on now, I’ve had enough
I am most annoyed, I’m getting tough.
I’m going to scream till I turn blue.
There’s no such thing as your man flu!”
Achoo! Achoo! Achoo!

Andrew Croft

WHITE VAN DRIVER

White van driver! You'd better look out.
White van driver, when he's about.
He's texting the girlfriend, phoning the wife.
Fiddling with his iPad all while he drives.
White van drivers are all the same - some dodgy
geezer, White van - no name!
He's eating a burger, it's double cheese.
Coke in the other hand, driving with his knees.
Then he's parked in a lay-by, feet on the dash.
Smoking a joint, flicking the ash.
Spies a cop car, he's off in a flash.
Winds down the window and throws out his stash.
White van drivers are all the same - some dodgy
geezer, White van - no name!
Ignores the crossings, parking askew.
Cutting up cyclists and taxi drivers too!
Window down, throws his fags on the road,
He's a white van driver with an unknown load.
He's up at the cross roads - is it left or right?
No indicators, one brake light.
I'm getting up close now there's a sign on the back.
Says "How's my driving?"
F in crap!

Andrew Croft

The old Town of Stamford has a tale to be told,
Many stories abound that will never grow old.
Two thousand years of history are well salted down
With these Legends of Stamford Town.
Here was the World's First University in BC 863,
Built by brave King Bladud, ruled by Christianity.
When Hengist beat the Picts and Scots in AD 449
He built this first Saxon Town of that time.

So let's ring St Peter's Bell again,
Tell the World we're all insane - halfway up the hill!
That Legendary Wall of Brass
Through which no enemy could pass,
Brazenose Knocker marks it still.
Stamford was built it in a day by The Saxons
(so they say)
Who put St Peter's on the Hill?
Some say that Boadicea never showed her face
around here, And some claim she lives here still!

The old Town of Stamford has a tale to be told,
Many stories abound that will never grow old.
The fact and the fiction are well watered down
With these Legends of Stamford Town.
The rebel Brazenose College came in1334.
A breakaway from Oxford – but Ed. III then said,
"No more! Just pull the wool and run the Bull!"
As it chased him up and down.

Ann Blades the first Bull Queen has left her tankard for the town.

Ring St Peter's Bell again
Tell the World we're still insane.
We're only halfway up the hill!
That Legendary Wall of Brass
Through which no enemy could pass,
Brazenose Knocker marks it still.
It was built it in a day when The Saxons were away!
They put St Peter's on the Hill.
Some say that Boadicea never showed her face around here and some claim she never will!

There's a string of famous people that have all passed this way.
The poet John Clare, yes he was there and Cromwell for a day.
Cassandra King was last to swing in 1704.
And Daniel Lambert found dead in bed;
He wouldn't fit through the door.
This now famous Town of Stamford has many a new tale to be told.
Many stories still abound that will never grow old.
The fact and the fiction are still being written down
With these Legends of Stamford Town!

Andrew Croft